A HISTORY OF THE CIVIL RIGHTS MOVEMENT

M. LaVora Perry

TITLES IN THIS SERIES

A HISTORY OF THE CIVIL RIGHTS MOVEMENT

M. LaVora Perry

Mason Crest
Philadelphia

Mason Crest
370 Reed Road, Suite 302
Broomall, PA 19008
www.MasonCrest.com

CPSIA Compliance Information: Batch #MBC2012-12. For further information, contact Mason Crest at 1-866-MCP-Book.

First printing
1 3 5 7 9 8 6 4 2

Library of Congress Cataloging-in-Publication Data

Perry, M. LaVora.
 A history of the civil rights movement / M. LaVora Perry.
    p. cm. — (Major black contributions from emancipation to civil rights)
 Includes bibliographical references and index.
 ISBN 978-1-4222-2382-6 (hc)
 ISBN 978-1-4222-2395-6 (pb)
 1. African Americans—Civil rights—History—20th century—Juvenile literature.
 2. Civil rights movements—History—20th century—Juvenile literature.
 3. United States—Race relations—Juvenile literature. I. Title.
 E185.61.P434 2012
 323.1196'07309046—dc23
                              2011051952

Picture credits: Library of Congress: 3, 8, 11, 14, 16, 17, 20, 22, 23, 28, 32, 34, 36, 39, 41, 42, 44, 46, 47, 48, 50, 55, 58; courtesy Lyndon B. Johnson Presidential Library: 51; National Archives: 23; © 2012 Photos.com, a division of Getty Images: 12; Danny E Hooks / Shutterstock.com: 7; Wikimedia Commons: 38.

Author's Note: For answering my questions, thank you Rhonda Y. Williams, Ph D., Case Western Reserve University's director. Also, thank you to Nancy Todd Noches and Ramon Todd Noches for sharing your rich history with me. Thanks to Cheryl Brown Henderson for helping me find the Nocheses. Big love and thanks to Cedric, Nia, Jarod, Jahci for your love and patience and to Daddy and Ma, Elder Rudolph Perry, Sr. and Mattie M. Perry for everything.

TABLE OF CONTENTS

INTRODUCTION

Dr. Marc Lamont Hill

It is impossible to tell the story of America without telling the story of Black Americans. From the struggle to end slavery, all the way to the election of the first Black president, the Black experience has been a window into America's own movement toward becoming a "more perfect union." Through the tragedies and triumphs of Blacks in America, we gain a more full understanding of our collective history and a richer appreciation of our collective journey. This book series, MAJOR BLACK CONTRIBUTIONS FROM EMANCIPATION TO CIVIL RIGHTS, spotlights that journey by showing the many ways that Black Americans have been a central part of our nation's development.

In this series, we are reminded that Blacks were not merely objects of history, swept up in the winds of social and political inevitability. Rather, since the end of legal slavery, Black men and women have actively fought for their own rights and freedoms. It is through their courageous efforts (along with the efforts of allies of all races) that Blacks are able to enjoy ever increasing levels of inclusion in American democracy. Through this series, we learn the names and stories of some of the most important contributors to our democracy.

But this series goes far beyond the story of slavery to freedom. The books in this series also demonstrate the various contributions of Black Americans to the nation's social, cultural, technological, and intellectual growth. While these books provide new and deeper insights into the lives and stories of familiar figures like Martin Luther King, Michael Jordan, and Oprah Winfrey, they also introduce readers to the contributions of countless heroes who have often been pushed to the margins of history. In reading this series, we are able to see that Blacks have been key contributors across every field of human endeavor.

Although this is a series about Black Americans, it is important and necessary reading for everyone. While readers of color will find enormous purpose and pride in uncovering the history of their ancestors, these books should also create similar sentiments among readers of all races and ethnicities. By understanding the rich and deep history of Blacks, a group often ignored or marginalized in history, we are reminded that everyone has a story. Everyone has a contribution. Everyone matters.

The insights of these books are necessary for creating deeper, richer, and more inclusive classrooms. More importantly, they remind us of the power and possibility of individuals of all races, places, and traditions. Such insights not only allow us to understand the past, but to create a more beautiful future.

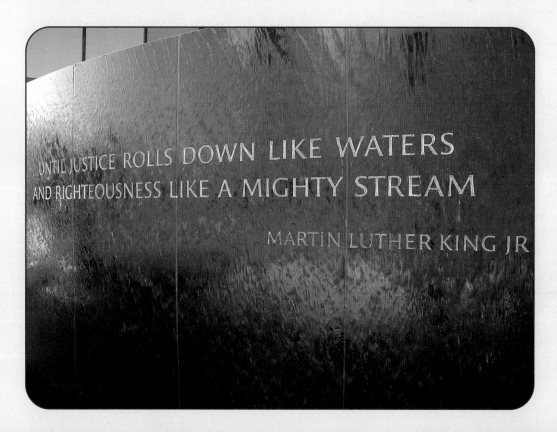

The Reverend Martin Luther King Jr. waves to a crowd of approximately 250,000 people after delivering his historic "I Have a Dream" speech on August 28, 1963. King's speech from the steps of the Lincoln Memorial was one of the highlights of the March on Washington for Jobs and Freedom, a key symbolic moment of the Civil Rights Movement.

HOW THE MOVEMENT BEGAN

The term *civil rights* refers to the personal liberties and legal rights that all individuals enjoy as citizens or residents of a country. For example, all residents of the United States have the right to express their opinions freely, to follow the religion of their choosing, and to peacefully protest government policies with which they disagree. Those rights are guaranteed by the First Amendment to the U.S. Constitution. All American citizens enjoy equal protection of the laws. This means that one group of people cannot legally be denied privileges or rights that other people in similar circumstances have. The Fourteenth Amendment guarantees equal treatment under the law.

The American tradition of government places great emphasis on the importance of civil rights. Yet the nation has been far from perfect in living up to its ideals. Throughout much of American history, black people were prevented from exercising the same rights and enjoying the same privileges as others. While slavery existed (from the early 1600s until 1865), enslaved African Americans had no rights. They couldn't be citizens. Under the law, they were property. The children of slaves also became property. Slave owners had the legal right to do almost anything they wished with their slaves.

Even after slavery ended, African Americans continued to suffer unfair treatment. In the South, a web of laws and social rules was put in place to prevent blacks from becoming equal members of society. This system of racial discrimination was known as Jim Crow. It barred black people from using the same public facilities as whites. For example, blacks weren't allowed to stay in hotels where whites stayed. They couldn't get served in restaurants where whites ate. They had to ride on "colored only" train cars. Black children had to go to separate schools. In almost every case, the facilities set aside for African Americans were inferior to those used by whites.

Laws that required racial segregation (the separation of blacks and whites) in public places were only part of the story. Southern states also established rules that made it impossible for most African Americans to vote. This effectively stopped the black community from changing Jim Crow through the political process. Jim Crow was also preserved through informal means. Black people who challenged the system faced the threat of violence from their white neighbors. And violence against African Americans was rarely punished when committed by whites.

Conditions for African Americans were worst in the South. But racial segregation existed in other parts of the country as well. And for many decades the federal (national) government did nothing to address the injustices.

Finally, in the middle of the 20th century, the civil rights movement began chipping away at the foundations of Jim Crow. The civil rights movement was a wide-ranging struggle for equality under the law. It was waged by tens of thousands of African Americans. A few were or would become famous leaders, such as Martin Luther King Jr. Most, however, were ordinary men, women, and youths who had the courage to stand up against injustice. White people, too, joined the civil rights movement.

Civil rights activists used a variety of tactics. They challenged Jim Crow laws in the courts. They held marches and demonstrations. They engaged in civil disobedience, refusing to obey unfair laws and regulations. They organized drives to register African-American voters.

The path toward equality was difficult. Every time African Americans took a step forward, whites who wanted to maintain racial segregation

For many years in the United States, African Americans suffered discrimination because of their race. (Left) A "colored" water fountain outside the courthouse of a North Carolina town. (Bottom) A black man climbs the steps to the "colored" entrance at the rear of a movie theater in Mississippi. The lower door is labled "white men only."

pushed back. Civil rights activists were attacked and beaten. Some lost their lives. But between the mid-1950s and the mid-1960s, the legal structure of Jim Crow was dismantled. Laws enacted by the federal government banned racial segregation and removed obstacles that had prevented African Americans from exercising the right to vote. At last, after centuries

Slaves pick cotton on a Southern plantation, 1850s. When the Civil War began in 1861, nearly 4 million African Americans were held in slavery.

of slavery and Jim Crow segregation, all of the nation's black people were promised equality under the law.

THE STAIN OF SLAVERY

Slavery has been referred to as America's "original sin." Between the 17th century and the first decade of the 19th century, hundreds of thousands of African captives were brought in chains to the area that would become the United States.

All of the 13 colonies that fought for independence from Great Britain during the Revolutionary War permitted slavery. The American Revolution was inspired by the principles of liberty and equality. As the Declaration of Independence proclaimed in 1776, "We hold these Truths to be self-evident, that all men are created equal, that they are endowed by their Creator with certain unalienable Rights, that among these are Life, Liberty, and the pursuit of Happiness."

However, the nation's Founding Fathers failed to extend the same "unalienable Rights" to slaves. The U.S. Constitution, drafted in 1787, banned the bringing of more slaves into the country after 1808. But it didn't free slaves who were already in the United States. And it didn't prevent the descendants of these slaves from being held in slavery.

During the 1790s and early 1800s, most of the northern states passed laws that gradually eliminated slavery. Slave labor wasn't vital in the northern states, whose economies were based on small-scale farming and manufacturing. As the decades passed, a growing movement in the North sought to get rid of slavery from the entire country. The campaign to end slavery was called abolitionism.

In the southern states, however, slavery was deeply entrenched. The South's economy was based on agriculture. Crops like tobacco, sugar, rice, and especially cotton were grown on large plantations. Slaves provided the cheap labor that made these plantations profitable. Many white southerners considered any attempt to end or limit slavery as an attack on their way of life.

From 1820 on, the issue of slavery caused a deepening rift between the

North and the South. A series of political compromises kept the nation together. But attitudes on both sides were hardening.

THE CIVIL WAR

Tensions finally boiled over after Abraham Lincoln was elected president in 1860. Lincoln was against slavery. He was determined not to let it spread into new areas as the United States expanded. But Lincoln had been careful not to promise to end slavery where it already existed. Nevertheless, seven southern states seceded, or withdrew, from the United States between December 1860 and February 1861. They formed their own government, called the Confederate States of America, or simply the Confederacy.

On April 12, 1861, Confederate forces fired on Fort Sumter, a U.S. government post in the harbor of Charleston, South Carolina. The attack—and Lincoln's determination to put down the southern rebellion—prompted four more states to join the Confederacy. The Civil War was under way.

The war's outcome would have enormous consequences. If the Confederacy won, the nation would probably be split permanently. Slavery would continue in the South. If, however, the war was won by the Union (the

An African-American soldier guards a row of cannons in Virginia, 1865. During the Civil War, about 186,000 African Americans fought for the Union Army.

states that remained in the United States), the country would be reunited. And the 4 million African Americans held in slavery would be freed.

The Civil War was the bloodiest conflict in American history. In four years of fighting, more than 600,000 men would lose their lives from all causes. These included almost 40,000 black soldiers. They were among the 180,000 African Americans who had joined the Union army to fight for the cause of freedom.

The Civil War finally ended in 1865. The Union had won, and much of the South was in ruins.

RECONSTRUCTION

On April 14, 1861, less than a week after the surrender of the largest Confederate army, an assassin shot President Lincoln. The president died the following day.

Upon Lincoln's death, Vice President Andrew Johnson became president. Johnson, a southerner from Tennessee, would be in charge of managing Reconstruction. This was the name given to the reorganization of the defeated Confederate states.

One of the first and most important tasks of Reconstruction was to officially abolish slavery. This was done by means of the Thirtenth Amendment to the U.S. Constitution. Ratified, or formally adopted, in December 1865, it banned slavery and "involuntary servitude."

But by 1866, all the states of the former Confederacy had moved to enact "Black Codes." These laws severely restricted the rights of African Americans in the South. In some states, for example, former slaves were required to sign annual labor contracts that committed them to working from sunup to sundown, six days a week, on a plantation. Wages were very low. African Americans who didn't sign a labor contract could be arrested and auctioned off to a planter. Those who left their plantation without permission could also be arrested. Black children could be taken from their families to work.

President Johnson saw nothing wrong with the Black Codes. Johnson wanted to limit the influence of newly freed slaves. "White men alone must

President Andrew Johnson did not want to grant the rights of citizenship to African Americans who were freed after the Civil War. His opposition to the laws passed by those who supported black citizenship led to his impeachment trial in the U.S. Senate.

manage the South," he declared.

But the Black Codes sparked widespread outrage in the North. It seemed clear that white southerners were trying to keep African Americans in a condition of "involuntary servitude." The U.S. Congress was determined to stop this. In April 1866, over the objection of President Johnson, Congress passed the Civil Rights Act of 1866. It granted equal rights of citizenship without regard to race. Federal troops in the South would help ensure that the law was enforced.

Congress sought to further guarantee the rights of African Americans with two additional amendments to the Constitution. The Fourteenth Amendment gave blacks citizenship and said that states couldn't deny anyone equal protection under the law. The amendment was passed by Congress in 1866 and ratified in 1868. The Fifteenth Amendment, passed by Congress in 1869, was ratified the following year. It said that no citizen could be denied the right to vote because of race or because he had previously been a slave.

Reconstruction appeared to signal the beginning of a brighter future for African Americans. Blacks enjoyed new educational opportunities. Some bought land and started businesses. Most important, African Americans won election to public office at the local, state, and national levels. With political power, blacks could ensure that civil rights remained a focus. There were eight African-American members of the U.S. Congress—seven in the House of Representatives and one in the Senate—when the Civil

Rights Act of 1875 was passed. The law said that "all persons within the jurisdiction of the United States shall be entitled to the full and equal and enjoyment of the accommodations, advantages, facilities, and privileges of inns, public [transportation] on land or water, theaters, and other places of public amusement."

THE RISE OF JIM CROW

Unfortunately, the period of African-American political empowerment under Reconstruction was brief. In 1876, the U.S. presidential elections led to a bitter dispute. Democrat Samuel Tilden and Republican Rutherford B. Hayes both claimed victory. Early in 1877, the Democratic and Republican parties struck a deal to resolve the dispute. The Democrats agreed to accept Hayes as president. In return, the Republicans promised to withdraw all federal troops from the South and end Reconstruction policies.

The southern states quickly began passing and enforcing Jim Crow laws. Forbidding African Americans from using the same trains, hotels, and other public facilities as whites seemed like a clear violation of the Civil Rights Act of 1875. But in 1883, the Supreme Court of the United States—the final authority on

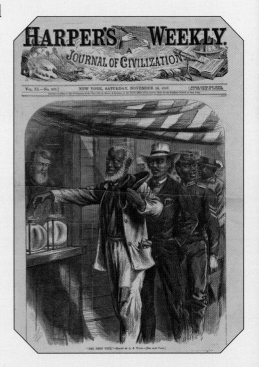

This illustration on the cover of *Harper's Weekly*, a popular magazine of the 1860s and 1870s, shows a line of African-American men preparing to cast ballots in an election. The first man is dressed as a laborer, the second is dressed as a businessman, the third is wearing a Union army uniform, and the fourth appears to be dressed as a farmer. The Fifteenth Amendment to the U.S. Constitution, ratified in 1870, made it illegal to deny a citizen the right to vote based on that person's "race, color, or previous condition of servitude." However, during the 1880s and 1890s states in the South began passing Jim Crow laws that effectively prevented blacks from voting.

what is and isn't permitted under the U.S. Constitution—struck down the Civil Rights Act. The justices declared that Congress didn't have the authority under the 14th Amendment to grant African Americans equal protection under the laws. Only state and local governments, the Supreme Court said, could do that.

Meanwhile, southern states were also finding ways to get around the 15th Amendment. That amendment made it unlawful to deny a person the right to vote based on race or previous status as a slave. But poll taxes prevented many black people from voting. Poor African Americans couldn't afford these special taxes, which had to be paid before a person was eligible to vote. Southern states also imposed literacy tests as a requirement for voting. Many African Americans didn't know how to read and write, because they had no formal education. So literacy tests effectively blocked them from voting. Of course, many poor whites couldn't afford to pay a poll tax and couldn't read or write either. Seven southern states would eventually solve this problem with a "grandfather clause." This exempted any man from having to pay the poll tax or pass a literacy test if he had an ancestor who'd been eligible to vote before 1867. No blacks fell into that category, but almost all whites did.

Some civil rights activists, black as well as white, challenged racial segregation in the South. One such group, organized in Louisiana, called itself the "Citizens' Committee to Test the Constitutionality of the Separate Car Act."

A Louisiana law passed in 1890 required railroads in the state to have separate train cars for white and black passengers. On June 7, 1892, a 30-year-old shoemaker and member if the Citizens' Committee boarded an East Louisiana Railroad train in New Orleans and took a seat in the whites-only car. Homer Plessy looked white. Seven of his eight great-grandparents were white. But under the law, a single drop of "black" blood made a person black. Plessy informed the conductor of his African-American ancestry and refused to leave the whites-only car. He was arrested.

In court, Plessy's lawyer argued that his client's civil rights—primarily those guaranteed under the 14th Amendment—had been violated. The trial judge, John H. Ferguson, rejected this argument. Ferguson found Plessy guilty of violating the Separate Car Act and ordered him to pay a $25 fine.

Plessy appealed the decision. But the Louisiana State Supreme Court sided with Ferguson. After another appeal, the case landed before the U.S. Supreme Court.

On May 18, 1896, the Supreme Court delivered its decision in the case known as *Plessy v. Ferguson*. By a 7–1 majority, the Court found that Louisiana's Separate Car Act didn't go against the Constitution. The justices admitted that the purpose of the 14th Amendment "was undoubtedly to enforce the absolute equality of the two races before the law." But, in the Court's opinion, the amendment

> could not have been intended to abolish distinctions based upon color, or to enforce social, as distinguished from political, equality, or a commingling of the two races upon terms unsatisfactory to either. Laws permitting, and even requiring, their separation, in places where they are liable to be brought into contact, do not necessarily imply the inferiority of either race to the other.

In other words, the 14th Amendment's requirement of equality before the law didn't mean that African Americans were entitled to use the same public facilities as whites. It only meant that blacks had to be provided with public facilities that were similar to the ones whites used. "Separate but equal" treatment of the races, the Court said, was perfectly legal.

With the *Plessy v. Ferguson* decision, Jim Crow had the legal blessing of the Supreme Court. Throughout the South, and sometimes even in other states, more laws were passed to enforce racial segregation. But the idea that the separate accommodations provided to blacks were equal to those enjoyed by whites was fiction. Jim Crow ensured that African Americans remained second-class citizens. Nearly 60 years would pass before the civil rights movement began to change the situation.

During the first half of the 20th century, Jim Crow laws in many southern states legally segregated whites and blacks, as the photos on this page, which were taken in the 1940s, show. (Top) This cafe in Durham, North Carolina, has separate entrances and seating areas for whites and blacks. (Bottom left) Blacks are required to stand behind white passengers while waiting for a bus at the terminal in Memphis, Tennessee.

Racial discrimination was not confined to the South during this time. In the northern states, many African Americans were unable to get a decent education or job because of racism.

THE CIVIL RIGHTS MOVEMENT TAKES HOLD

By the early 1900s, Jim Crow was thoroughly entrenched in the South. African-American leaders disagreed on what course to take. Some were willing to accept segregation, at least in the short term. The black community, they said, should concentrate on self-improvement through hard work and education. Equality under the law would come eventually. The most famous advocate of this viewpoint was the educator Booker T. Washington.

Other black leaders demanded that African Americans receive full civil rights immediately. W. E. B. Du Bois was perhaps the most influential champion of this position. Born in Massachusetts in 1868, Du Bois became the first African American to receive a doctoral degree from Harvard University. He wrote widely about racism and, in 1905, helped found an organization called the Niagara Movement. It brought together leading African-American intellectuals, writers, and journalists. The Niagara Movement had limited influence. Its membership never grew to more than a few hundred.

But Du Bois helped found a much more significant civil rights organization. In August 1908, a deadly race riot tore through Abraham Lincoln's hometown of Springfield, Illinois. Shocked by the violence, about 60 concerned citizens met in New York City the following February. Du Bois was

Booker T. Washington (1856–1915) believed it was critical for African Americans to become educated so they could succeed economically in the post–Civil War South.

one of seven African Americans in attendance. The meeting led to the formation of the National Association for the Advancement of Colored People (NAACP). Its members were determined to see all Americans enjoy equal protection under the law.

The NAACP took a multi-pronged approach to the struggle for equality. Du Bois launched and was the longtime editor of the organization's magazine, called *The Crisis*. In its pages, talented writers chronicled the evils of racism and made the case for civil rights. The NAACP undertook a campaign against lynching. It organized protests against a popular 1915 motion picture, *The Birth of a Nation*, which glorified the Ku Klux Klan. The NAACP also mounted legal challenges to racist laws.

In 1940, the NAACP Legal Defense Fund was founded. Headed by a young African-American lawyer named Thurgood Marshall, the Legal Defense Fund would fight segregation in the courts.

W.E.B. Du Bois (1868–1963) was a major scholar and activist of the early 20th century. He helped to found the National Association for the Advancement of Colored People (NAACP) in 1909. As editor of the NAACP's magazine, *The Crisis*, he attacked racism and oppression.

INTEGRATING THE MILITARY

Meanwhile, the struggle for civil rights was being waged in other arenas as well. In 1941, A. Philip Randolph, leader of a black labor union called the Brotherhood of Sleeping Car Porters, planned a 100,000-person march on Washington, D.C. Its purpose was to protest racial segregation in the American armed forces and discriminatory hiring practices in the defense industry.

To avert the huge demonstration, President Franklin D. Roosevelt signed Executive Order 8802. Issued on June 25, 1941, it prohibited employment discrimination in the defense industry. Roosevelt's executive order didn't address the other issue in question—segregation in the armed forces. Still, Randolph believed that progress had been made. He called off the protest march. The armed forces remained segregated.

During World War II—which the United States entered in December 1941 and which lasted until August 1945—African Americans served in segregated units. In many other ways, they were treated poorly. In 1947, Randolph and fellow activist Grant Reynolds decided to change the situation. They founded an organization dedicated to ending segregation in the U.S. military. In June 1948, after the group was renamed the League for

A machine gun crew made up of black and white soldiers with the 2nd Infantry Division watches North Korean troops, November 1950. Two years earlier, President Truman had issued an order desegregating the U.S. military.

Non-Violent Civil Disobedience Against Military Segregation, Randolph brought matters to a head. He informed President Harry S. Truman that blacks would refuse to be drafted into the military unless the armed forces were integrated.

On July 26, 1948, Truman signed Executive Order 9981. "It is hereby declared to be the policy of the President," the order stated, "that there shall be equality of treatment and opportunity for all persons in the armed services without regard to race, color, religion, or national origin." Randolph and his colleagues had helped end racial segregation in the military. That victory would provide momentum for the growing civil rights movement.

SCHOOL DESEGREGATION

During the 1930s the NAACP began working to end the "separate but equal" doctrine established by *Plessy v. Ferguson*. The NAACP Legal Defense and Educational Fund filed lawsuits demanding that the educational facilities provided for black students be made equal to those for whites. Some of these suits proved successful. The overall goal of the NAACP was to end legal segregation altogether.

In December 1952 there were five school segregation lawsuits awaiting review by the U.S. Supreme Court. They represented more than 150 plaintiffs who were from several different states. All challenged the lawfulness of racial segregation practices in the public school system. The Court consolidated all five cases under one name: *Oliver Brown et al. v. the Board of Education of Topeka, Kansas*.

NAACP attorneys, including Thurgood Marshall, presented their arguments in *Brown v. Board of Education* on December 9, 1952. The lawyers argued that school segregation violated the "equal protection clause" of the 14th Amendment. This clause prohibits states from denying citizens equal treatment under the law. To support their case, the lawyers presented evidence that segregated schools had a negative impact on African American students. The schools caused black children to believe they were not equal

Attorneys George E. C. Hayes (left), Thurgood Marshall (center), and James M. Nabrit (right) celebrate outside the U.S. Supreme Court building after the Court ruled in May 1954 that school segregation was unconstitutional. In 1967, Marshall (1908–1993) would become the first African American to serve as a Supreme Court justice.

to whites. Segregation laws in education resulted in a separate and unequal education for black children.

The Supreme Court heard the case again on two more occasions. In May 1954 it submitted its decision. The Court agreed that segregation in public

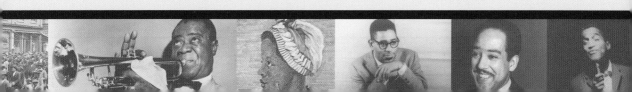

education violated the equal protection clause of the 14th Amendment. In announcing the unanimous decision, Chief Justice Earl Warren wrote:

> Segregation of white and colored children in public schools has a detrimental effect upon the colored children. The impact is greater when it has the sanction of the law. . . . We conclude that, in the field of public education, the doctrine of "separate but equal" has no place. Separate educational facilities are inherently unequal.

The Supreme Court ruled that racially segregated public schools were a violation of the U.S. Constitution. All public schools were ordered to desegregate.

THE CHALLENGE BEGINS

The *Brown v. Board of Education* decision gave the civil rights movement a defining victory. However, the process of desegregating schools would take determination and time. The order to integrate public schools met with heavy resistance from Southern whites. It wasn't uncommon for resolute segregationists to refuse to integrate their public schools. Opposition came from public schools all over the South, from Texas and Kentucky to Tennessee and Mississippi.

Resistance took many forms. Rather than integrate, some white-dominated school boards closed schools. In other cases, mobs of angry whites prevented African American students from attempting to enter all-white schools. Some government officials openly opposed integration. They refused to enforce the ruling. It would be many years before public schools in the United States were integrated.

The Murder of Emmett Till

During the 1950s, leaders like Bayard Rustin and Martin Luther King advocated nonviolence as a way to draw attention to the plight of African Americans in the South. However, some whites had no qualms about using violence as a way to deter blacks from speaking out. African Americans were expected to "keep in their place"—to be subservient to white Americans. In the South, racist whites could hurt or even kill blacks and expect to get away with it. Police departments and local courts were controlled by whites, and they rarely prosecuted whites who attacked blacks.

In one famous case, a 14-year-old African-American boy named Emmett Till traveled by train from Chicago to visit his great-uncle Moses Wright in Money, Mississippi. On August 24, 1955, the boy spoke to a white woman, Carolyn Bryant, who was working at a grocery store. She was so upset that she told her husband, Roy Bryant. On the night of August 28, Roy Bryant and his half-brother John W. Milam drove to Moses Wright's house and took Till. They met a group of other white men, who beat Till severely, shot him in the head, and dumped his body in the Tallahatchie River. Till's mutilated body was found three days later.

The horrible murder drew national attention. The body was returned to Chicago, where 50,000 people attended Emmitt Till's funeral. His mother Mamie Till Bradley insisted on an open casket. She said, "everybody needed to know what had happened to Emmett Till." Photographs of Till's mutilated body were published in national magazines. Despite the outrage, on September 23, 1955, an all-white, all-male jury found Bryant and Milam not guilty, and freed them.

In January 1956, *Look* magazine published an article titled "The Shocking Story of Approved Killing in Mississippi." In it, Bryant and Milam told exactly how they had murdered Emmett Till. Mamie Till wrote to the president and the FBI, asking them to investigate, but they never answered. Nonetheless, the publicity surrounding the murder of Emmett Till became a symbol of the unfair status of blacks in the South.

On December 1, 1955, Rosa Parks was arrested and charged with disorderly conduct in Montgomery, Alabama, for refusing to give up her bus seat to a white passenger. Her arrest and $14 fine for violating a city ordinance led African-American bus riders and others to boycott the Montgomery city buses. The boycott lasted for one year and brought the Civil Rights Movement worldwide attention.

THE MONTGOMERY BUS BOYCOTT

The *Brown v. Board of Education* decision did not put an end to segregation in other public areas. There were still whites-only restaurants, movie theaters, and restrooms. Many states and cities had laws that punished businesses that did not provide separate facilities for black and white customers. Some state laws prohibited interracial marriages. Others imposed segregation practices in public transportation.

In Montgomery, Alabama, city law required passengers on buses to be segregated. Whites took seats in the front rows. African Americans had to take seats in the back of the bus. If the bus became full, all the blacks in the row nearest the white section had to get up from their seats. This would create a new row for white passengers. If there were no seats available for them, African American riders were supposed to stand. In addition, black passengers often had to board the bus in the front door to pay the fare. But then they had to exit the bus and reenter using the rear door.

NAACP lawyers continued to challenge segregation in the courts. But in the 1950s, African Americans also used a tactic called civil disobedience to draw attention to the civil rights cause.

TAKING A STAND—SEATED

On March 2, 1955, in Montgomery, Alabama, police officers arrested 15-

year-old Claudette Colvin for refusing to give a white passenger her bus seat. On October 21, officers arrested 18-year-old Mary Louise Smith for the same "crime."

Then on Thursday, December 1, 1955, the most famous act of American civil disobedience occurred. It involved 42-year-old Rosa Parks, who was leaving work when she got onto a Montgomery bus. Parks sat down in the first row of the bus's "colored" section—the seats from the middle to the back. After passengers filled all the seats, a white man was left standing. Another black man sat by Parks, in the window seat. Two black women sat across the aisle from Parks. The bus driver, James F. Blake, told the four black riders, "Let me have those seats." No one moved. Blake said "Y'all better make it light on yourselves and let me have those seats."

The man and two women stood. But Parks scooted into the window seat. In her autobiography *My Story* she said, "I could not see how standing up was going to 'make it light' on me. The more we gave in, [the worse they treated us]."

Parks told Blake that she would not stand. He said, "I'm going to have you arrested." She replied "You may do that."

Two police officers entered the bus. One asked Parks why she wouldn't stand. She answered, "Why do you all push us around?" The police officers took Parks to jail.

BUS BOYCOTT BEGINS

Within a few hours of Rosa Parks's arrest, Jo Ann Robinson heard the news. Robinson, an English professor at the all-black Alabama State College in Montgomery, was president of the Women's Political Council (WPC), a civil rights group of 300 women. For years, the WPC and other groups had talked about boycotting Montgomery's buses. In 1953, Robinson had sent a letter to the mayor of Montgomery, William Gayle, warning that African Americans would stop riding the buses if the abuses didn't stop. Robinson knew that African-Americans riders were important to the bus company. Three-quarters of the bus passengers were black, and if they stopped riding the bus company would lose a lot of money.

Understanding Nonviolent Protest

In February 1956, a New York civil rights group called the Congress of Racial Equality (CORE) sent one of its leading members, Bayard Rustin, to Montgomery. Rustin was a member of a religious group called the Quakers, who strongly opposed war and fighting. Rustin had been a proponent of nonviolent protest since the 1940s. He had spent time with Indian leader Mohandas K. Gandhi, who had effectively used civil disobedience to help India gain its freedom from Great Britain. Rustin had also studied the methods of 19th century American abolitionist Henry David Thoreau. In Montgomery, Rustin helped to trained Martin Luther King and others boycott leaders in how to use nonviolent tactics.

Civil disobedience occurs when a person refuses to obey laws that the person feels are unfair. A key part of this tactic is that the person cannot fight back or resist the consequence of breaking the law, such as being thrown in jail. This is known as "nonviolent resistance," or nonviolence. The idea behind nonviolent civil disobedience is that when large groups of people allow themselves to be punished for refusing to accept unjust laws, their action draws public attention to the unfair situation. As the government realizes that people would rather go to prison than live under the existing laws and conditions, it is pressured to make changes.

At first, it was hard for civil rights leaders to explain why nonviolent civil disobedience would be effective. "We had to make it clear that nonviolent resistance is not a method of cowardice. It does resist," explained King in 1957. "The nonviolent resister does not seek to humiliate or defeat the opponent but to win his friendship and understanding. This was always a cry that we had to set before people that our aim is not to defeat the white community . . . but to win the friendship of all of the persons who had perpetrated this system in the past. The end of violence or the aftermath of violence is bitterness. The aftermath of nonviolence is reconciliation and the creation of a beloved community. A boycott is never an end within itself. It is merely a means to awaken a sense of shame within the oppressor but the end is reconciliation, the end is redemption."

Early in the morning of December 2, 1955, Robinson and three helpers met at Alabama State College. They printed 52,000 flyers on the college's mimeograph (copying) machine. The flyers told African Americans about Rosa Parks's arrest, and that her trial was scheduled for Monday, December 5. "Please stay off all buses Monday," read the flyers. WPC members posted flyers everywhere. The Sunday issue of the *Montgomery Advertiser*, a newspaper for the city's African-American community, reproduced Robinson's message on the front page.

On December 5, Parks walked up the steps to the courthouse with E.D. Nixon, the head of the local NAACP chapter, and her lawyers Fred Gray and Charles Langford. About 500 supporters lined the steps as she passed. In court, the judge fined Parks $10 for disorderly conduct, plus $4 in court costs. That day, some 40,000 African Americans walked or found alternate ways to get to school or work. They refused to ride the Montgomery buses.

The front page of the *Montgomery Advertiser* from December 6, 1955, includes a story about the meeting at the Holt Street Baptist Church.

The bus boycott was so successful that local leaders decided to continue it. On the afternoon of December 5 a group called the Montgomery Improvement Association (MIA) was formed. They chose a Baptist minister who was new in town to lead the group: 26-year-old Martin Luther King Jr. That night, more than 5,000 African Americans crowded into the Holt Street Baptist Church to learn more about the boycott. Reverend King spoke to the crowd. "I want it to be known that we're going to work with grim and bold determination to gain justice on the buses in this city. And we are not wrong," he said. "If we are wrong, the Supreme Court of this nation is wrong. If we are wrong, the Constitution of the United States is wrong. If we are wrong, God Almighty is wrong."

CONTINUING THE BOYCOTT

Over the next year, tens of thousands of African Americans—mostly women who worked as housekeepers, babysitters, and cooks—boycotted the Montgomery city buses. They walked or rode bicycles, mules, and horses. To get to work each day, about 30,000 boycotters rode in carpools. Some of the cars were driven by white women.

King and other MIA leaders, such as Nixon and the Reverend Ralph Abernathy, told the Montgomery Bus Company the boycott would continue until the company agreed to treat African American riders with respect, allowed them to sit wherever they wanted, and hired more black drivers.

The Montgomery Bus Company lost a significant amount of money without black riders. Plus, businesses in Montgomery suffered also, because African Americans refused to ride buses to shop. But the black community suffered too. Some people who supported the boycott were fired from their jobs by white bosses. Sometimes blacks walking to work were threatened or attacked. Police stopped black carpool drivers and gave them tickets for minor traffic violations. People set off bombs at the homes of King and Nixon. King and other leaders were also arrested. Still, the boycott continued.

LEGAL CHALLENGE

As the boycott continued, Rosa Parks and four other women who had previously been arrested on Montgomery buses—Aurelia Browder, Susie McDonald, Claudette Colvin, and Mary Louise Smith— agreed to serve as plaintiffs in a lawsuit that challenged city and state segregation laws. The case was filed in U.S. district court in February 1956 by lawyer Fred Gray. He had assistance from NAACP lawyers, including Thurgood Marshall. The case became known as *Browder v. Gayle*. (Aurelia Browder was the lead petitioner, or first person named in the suit, and William Gayle was the mayor of Montgomery.)

The suit charged that Alabama's bus segregation laws violated the 14th Amendment of the U.S. Constitution. In June 1956 the U.S. district court

Bayard Rustin was one of the most influential leaders of the Civil Rights Movement. He is not as well known as other black leaders of the 1950s and 1960s because he preferred to work behind the scenes. He organized protests and boycotts, and allowed others to act as the public face of the movement.

ruled in favor of the plaintiffs. And on December 17, 1956, the U.S. Supreme Court agreed with the ruling that Alabama's segregation laws were unconstitutional.

Only after the Supreme Court had ruled were Montgomery civil rights activists willing to call off the bus boycott. It officially ended on December 20, 1956. The protest had lasted 381 days. The success of the Montgomery bus boycott was a critical point in the history of the civil rights movement, and helped make Martin Luther King Jr. and others who had been involved in the boycott into nationally known figures. Most importantly, the success of the bus boycott showed blacks that by working together, they could bring about change.

To make this happen, a regional organization was needed to help coordinate protests in the South. In January 1957, Martin Luther King and Bayard Rustin met with several dozen African-American ministers in Atlanta, Georgia. The activists agreed to for a group called the Southern Christian Leadership Council (SCLC). King became the group's first president, while Ella Josephine Baker, a former NAACP branch president, became the SCLC's executive secretary. The SCLC also included such well-known pastors as the Reverend Fred Shuttlesworth of Birmingham, the Reverend Joseph Lowery of Mobile, the Reverend Ralph Abernathy of Montgomery, and the Reverend C.K. Steele of Tallahassee.

The group soon issued a document stating that civil rights are essential to democracy, that segregation should end, and that all black people should oppose segregation nonviolently.

SIT-INs
AND FREEDOM RIDES

I n the South, racial segregation meant that managers of restaurants could refuse to serve blacks. It meant that water fountains and rest- rooms were labeled as for "Whites" or "Colored." It meant that whites and blacks did not share swimming pools, libraries, or other public places.

The SCLC, headquartered in Atlanta, Georgia, worked to end segrega- tion in all areas of society. Campaigns to end discrimination involved law- suits, boycotts of merchants, sit-ins, rallies, and marches. SCLC president Martin Luther King Jr., insisted on conducting challenges to segregation through nonviolence. This strategy of nonviolent resistance would help draw many members—black and white—into the civil rights movement.

TARGETING LUNCH COUNTERS

The strategy of nonviolence would prove crucial in desegregating American lunch counters. In most places in the South, blacks could not sit at the lunch counters of local department stores or neighborhood restaurants. As a routine practice, these businesses refused to serve food or beverages to African Americans.

In 1960, four young black men—Franklin McCain, Joseph McNeil, Ezell Blair Jr., and David Richmond—decided to challenge this discrimina-

Young African Americans, probably students at North Carolina Central Agriculture and Technical College, conduct a "sit-in" at a segregated Woolworth's lunch counter in Greensboro.

tion. They were freshmen at the blacks-only Agricultural and Technical State University in Greensboro, North Carolina. On February 1 the four entered the downtown F. W. Woolworth department store. The business catered to both blacks and whites. But the luncheon counter was open only to whites. The four black men made purchases in the store. They then sat down at the lunch counter and ordered food.

The white waitress told the men that she could not serve blacks. The manager asked them to leave. But the four stayed seated. They quietly waited at the counter until the store closed. And they returned the next day. This time they were accompanied by about 20 more students, including four women. Local newspapers and TV news programs reported the story.

On the third day, there were approximately 60 people participating in the sit-in. Among them were several African American female students from Bennett College. On the fourth day, three white female students from Greensboro Women's College joined the more than 300 students at the sit-in. A similar protest took place that day at the nearby S. H. Kress & Company retail store.

As news of the Greensboro protests spread, students organized sit-ins in other North Carolina cities and in other states. In some cases, African American students were joined by white students. Civil rights activist James Farmer later explained the importance of sit-ins:

> They symbolized a change in the mood of African American people. Up until then, we had accepted segregation—begrudgingly—but we had accepted it. . . . At long last after decades of acceptance, four freshman students at North Carolina A&T went into Woolworth and at the lunch counter they "sat-in." When told they would not be served, they refused to leave and this sparked a movement throughout the South.

THE SIT-IN MOVEMENT

In Nashville, Tennessee, 22-year-old Diane Nash was inspired by the Greensboro sit-in. Nash had grown up in Chicago, Illinois. Until she transferred from Howard University in Washington, D.C., to Fisk University in Nashville, she had not experienced the ugliness of segregation. She quickly became an activist. With John Lewis, she organized the Nashville Student Movement (NSM), which worked for the civil rights of blacks.

Nash and other NSM members had been planning to hold sit-in protests in Nashville. On February 13, 1960, she was one of 124 students who sat-in at lunch counters in downtown stores. She later explained:

> When the students in Greensboro sat in on February 1, we simply made plans to join their effort by sitting in at the same chains. . . . We were surprised and delighted to hear reports of other cities joining in the sit-ins. We started feeling the power of the idea whose time had come. We had no inkling that the movement would become so widespread.

On February 27, 1960, Nash led students to a third sit-in at a Woolworth's lunch counter in downtown Nashville. A group of young white thugs attacked the sitters. The police were called to break up the fight. They arrested Diane Nash and 80 other black students, but did not detain the white instigators. Two days later, a judge fined the black students $50.

Diane Nash

Nash told the judge that rather than pay the fine, the students would go to jail to protest the injustice of segregation. The judge sentenced the students to 30 days in jail.

Nashville Mayor Ben West agreed to free the students if they stopped the sit-ins. He promised to form a racially integrated group to decide how to end segregation. The students agreed to not sit-in at lunch counters. But when the mayor's group did little about segregation, students resumed the sit-ins. They also boycotted stores and protested in front of the courthouse.

In the morning of April 19, 1960, a bomb exploded at the Nashville home of Alexander Looby, a lawyer who had represented students arrested in the sit-ins. Fortunately, Looby and his wife were unhurt. The next day, thousands of angry students marched to Nashville's city hall to confront Mayor West. As television cameras and reporters watched, Diane Nash asked, "Mayor West, do you feel it is wrong to [treat a person unfairly just because of] race or color?" West answered yes, that unfair treatment was wrong. The headline on the front page of the *Nashville Tennessean* the following day announced, "Mayor Says Integrate Counters." Within three weeks, managers of six downtown lunch counters allowed African Americans to sit wherever they pleased.

It took Woolworth's management much longer to change its segregation policy. Six months after the first Greensboro sit-in, on July 25, 1960, Woolworth officials ordered its store chains to desegregate. But the power of the sit-ins reached further. Similar protests that occurred in nine states eventually led to the passage of legislation that ended segregation policies in restaurants, theaters, and concert halls.

FREEDOM RIDERS

In April 1960 Diane Nash and John Lewis attended a meeting organized by an SCLC official named Ella Baker. A supporter of grassroots organiz-

Ella Josephine Baker was active in the civil rights movement for more than 50 years. As an NAACP activist, she worked with many important civil rights leaders, including W. E. B. Du Bois, Bayard Rustin, Thurgood Marshall, Martin Luther King, Rosa Parks, and Diane Nash. Baker helped organize the SCLC in 1957 and the SNCC in 1960.

ing and youth activism, Baker was reaching out to leaders of the sit-in protests. More than 200 black students participated in the conference. From that meeting the Student Nonviolent Coordinating Committee (SNCC) was created. This student-run organization would go on to play a major role in coordinating sit-ins and other civil rights actions, including Freedom Rides.

The Freedom Rides were meant to test laws in southern states that mandated segregation. Such laws were supposed to be illegal. In 1946 the U.S. Supreme Court had ruled in *Morgan v. Commonwealth of Virginia* that was unconstitutional to segregate bus and train passengers traveling between states. That decision had been affirmed in 1955 by the Interstate Commerce Commission, the federal agency that oversaw transportation between the states. But in the South, local authorities continued to ban white and blacks from sitting together when traveling in buses and trains. The waiting rooms and restrooms were still marked "White" and "Colored."

In December 1960, the U.S. Supreme Court overturned a lower court's conviction of an African-American student for trespassing in a bus terminal restaurant labeled for whites only. In the case *Boynton v. Virginia*, the Supreme Court affirmed that because racial segregation in public transportation was illegal, African

John Lewis

Americans had a legal right to be in any restaurant or bus terminal that served insterstate passengers.

In the months following the *Boynton v. Virginia* decision, some African Americans decided to test local policies regarding segregation in buses and bus stations throughout the South. This was the start of the Freedom Rides. The first one left Washington, D.C., on May 4, bound for New Orleans. It was organized and led by James L. Farmer, who had co-founded the Congress of Racial Equality in the 1940s. At first the Riders encountered little trouble, but they were brutally attacked and the bus firebombed when it reached Birmingham, Alabama.

> ═ *Did You Know?* ═
>
> On their trip, Freedom Riders sometimes sang, "Get on the bus, sit anyplace, 'cause Irene Morgan won her case." This was a reference to the landmark Supreme Court decision *Morgan v. Commonwealth of Virginia* (1946), which declared segregation of interstate transportation facilities illegal.

During the spring and summer of 1961, more than 400 people, both black and white, participated in Freedom Rides. Many were members of SNCC or CORE. These Freedom Riders often faced mobs of angry whites. Segregationists intercepted buses, pulled riders off, and beat them. In Birmingham, Ku Klux Klansmen used bats, iron pipes, and chains to beat a group of Freedom Riders that included John Lewis and a young white student named James Zwerg. Photographs of these brutal incidents shocked the nation. Those Freedom Riders who avoided attacks were often jailed for breaking local laws. Diane Nash, who helped organize the Freedom Rides, later said:

> If the Freedom Riders had been stopped as a result of violence, I strongly felt that the future of the movement was going to be cut short. The impression would have been that whenever a movement starts, all [you have to do] is attack it with massive violence and the blacks [will] stop.

That September the Kennedy administration called on the Interstate Commerce Commission to enforce the ban on segregation in trains and

Right: Members of the "Washington Freedom Riders Committee," enroute to Washington, D.C., hang signs from bus side windows to protest segregation as they travel through New York City, 1961.

Below: A map that was reproduced in newspapers showing the bus routes of the 1961 Freedom Rides through the South.

buses. New regulations were drafted that went into effect in November 1961. They overruled local segregation ordinances. Passengers were allowed to sit wherever they wanted on interstate buses and trains. The regulations also called for removal of "White" and "Colored" signs from terminals. Drinking fountains, restrooms, and waiting rooms were to be shared by everyone, regardless of skin color. This was an important victory for the Civil Rights Movement, although it would take years before facilities in the South were fully integrated.

Top: Alabama's segregationist governor, George Wallace, (left, in suit) blocks the entrance to the University of Alabama in an attempt to keep two African American students, Vivian Malone and James Hood, from enrolling in June 1963. Federal troops had to remove the governor so that the students could register.

Bottom left: New York policemen subdue a black man during a riot in Harlem, 1964. As tensions between black and white Americans rose, riots occurred in many cities during the 1960s.

FEDERAL LAWS PROTECT CIVIL RIGHTS

While the nonviolent example of the Freedom Rides helped with desegregation efforts, many in the South refused to accept that times were changing. Their attitudes were summed up by Alabama governor George Wallace, who in January 1963 declared that he would continue to oppose efforts by the federal government to force integration of public facilities in Alabama. Wallace's statement "I say segregation now, segregation tomorrow, segregation forever" would become a rallying cry for those opposed to African American civil rights.

In response, a Birmingham, Alabama, minister named Fred Shuttlesworth, who had helped to found the SCLC, asked Martin Luther King to get involved in protests against segregation in the city. At the time, Birmingham was one of the most segregated cities in America, and violence against African Americans was so common that the city had been nicknamed "Bombingham."

King wanted to bring Birmingham's racist policies to the nation's attention. In April 1963 he called for boycotts against businesses. Activists organized sit-ins and protest marches. Children and adults were encouraged to take part. By early May, hundreds of blacks had been arrested. One of them was King, who had been part of a protest march.

Medgar W. Evers (1925–1963) worked for the NAACP in Mississippi during the 1950s and 1960s. He investigated incidents of racial violence, led voter registration drives, and organized boycotts and protests against segregation. Evers was assassinated by a white man, Byron De La Beckwith, in 1963. In 1964 De La Beckwith was put on trial two times for the murder; both times, the all-white Mississippi jury would not vote to convict. In 1994, the case was re-opened. This time, De La Beckwith was finally convicted; he died in prison in 2001.

On April 16, while in jail, King wrote a letter meant to respond to criticism from some white religious leaders in Alabama. In his "Letter from a Birmingham Jail," which was later published, King explained why African-American activists were using civil disobedience tactics in order to bring about change:

> You express a great deal of anxiety over our willingness to break laws. This is certainly a legitimate concern. . . . One may well ask: "How can you advocate breaking some laws and obeying others?" The answer lies in the fact that there are two types of laws: just and unjust. I would be the first to advocate obeying just laws. One has not only a legal but a moral responsibility to obey just laws. Conversely, one has a moral responsibility to disobey unjust laws. I would agree with St. Augustine that "an unjust law is no law at all."

King was released from prison on bail after eight days. In the meantime, the protests in Birmingham continued. Civil rights protesters were met with force. Firemen battered them with high-pressure streams of water from fire hoses. Law enforcement officers set police dogs on crowds. Police pummeled individuals with clubs. Photographs and television footage of the attacks on peaceful protesters horrified most of the country.

President John F. Kennedy urged local government officials to meet with protest leaders. On May 10, 1963, Birmingham officials freed thousands of student prisoners. The officials promised to racially integrate public places, make sure African American job-seekers got fair treatment, and continue meeting with African-Americans to address their concerns. A month later, Kennedy gave a televised speech to the nation. He called for federal laws that would ensure all Americans, regardless of color, received equal treatment under the law.

> ═ *Did You Know?* ═
>
> Fred Shuttlesworth refered to the Birmingham protests in the spring of 1963 as "Project C." The "C" stood for "confrontation." The intent was to inspire a violent reaction from local police that would draw national attention to the problem of segregation.

MARCH ON WASHINGTON

Later in 1963, civil rights activists began planning a march on the U.S. capital, Washington, D.C. They wanted to send a message that African Americans deserved fair treatment. A union leader named A. Phillip Randolph and CORE activist Bayard Rustin organized the event, which was called the "March on Washington for Jobs and Freedom."

On August 28, 1963, more than 250,000 people marched from the Washington Monument to the Lincoln Memorial. At the steps of the Memorial, they listened to opera star Marian Anderson and gospel singer Mahalia Jackson. They heard several men, representing various civil rights organizations, give speeches. The one that would be best remembered was delivered by King. That day he gave his famous "I Have a Dream" speech, in which he spoke about his desire for peaceful integration:

> I have a dream that my four little children will one day live in a nation where they will not be judged by the color of their skin but by the content of their character. . . .
>
> This will be the day, this will be the day when all of God's children will be able to sing with new meaning, "My country 'tis of thee, sweet land of liberty, of thee I sing. Land where my fathers died, land of the Pilgrim's pride, from every mountainside, let freedom ring!"

And if America is to be a great nation, this must become true. And so let freedom ring from the prodigious hilltops of New Hampshire. Let freedom ring from the mighty mountains of New York. Let freedom ring from the heightening Alleghenies of Pennsylvania.

Let freedom ring from the snow-capped Rockies of Colorado. Let freedom ring from the curvaceous slopes of California.

But not only that; let freedom ring from Stone Mountain of Georgia.

Let freedom ring from Lookout Mountain of Tennessee.

Let freedom ring from every hill and molehill of Mississippi—from every mountainside.

Let freedom ring. And when this happens, and when we allow freedom to ring—when we let it ring from every village and every hamlet, from every state and every city, we will be able to speed up that day when all of God's children—black men and white men, Jews and Gentiles, Protestants and Catholics—will be able to join hands and sing in the words of the old Negro spiritual: "Free at last! Free at last! Thank God Almighty, we are free at last!"

NAACP executive secretary Roy Wilkins (second row, center) walks with other activists during the August 1963 "March on Washington for Jobs and Freedom." Wilkins (1901–1981) was an NAACP leader for more than 40 years.

Members of CORE lead a march in Washington, D.C., to draw attention to violence in the South. The photo they are carrying shows the 16th Street Baptist Church, where a bomb planted by white supremacists killed four young black girls in September 1963.

King's dream of peaceful integration seemed far off, however, as the violence resistance to integration continued throughout 1963. On September 15, 1963, four members of the Ku Klux Klan set off a bomb at the 16th Street Baptist Church in Birmingham, where King and others had planned the Birmingham campaign in the spring. Four young girls—11-year-old Denise McNair and 14-year-olds Addie Mae Collins, Carole Robertson, and Cynthia Wesley—were killed and 22 others were injured. It was the 27th bombing in Birmingham that year. The bombers would not be brought to justice for decades.

FREEDOM SUMMER

A year after the March on Washington, the Student Nonviolent Coordinating Committee began a major effort to register black voters in the South. At the time, many Southern blacks were denied the right to vote. This was particularly true in Mississippi. The state had the lowest African American voter registration in the country. In 1962, less than 7 percent of eligible black voters were registered.

If you lived in Mississippi in 1964 and you were black, it was not easy to vote. First you had to register at the courthouse. You had to fill out a long form with 20 questions. You had to copy any section of the state's constitution. Then you had to explain what it meant—in writing. Many blacks in Mississippi were poor and uneducated. Most of them couldn't qualify to vote. Because they weren't permitted to vote, African Americans could not decide who would represent them in the local, state, and national government. They could not elect African Americans or those who would work to end segregation and ensure civil rights for blacks.

SNCC decided to try to change that. Their project, called Freedom Summer, had many goals. The top goal was to help more blacks in Mississippi register to vote. Other goals were to open community centers, help black kids with reading and math, and start a new political party that would listen to the needs of African Americans.

College students from around the country—both black and white—volunteered to take part in the project. After a training session, the first group headed for Mississippi. Not long after that, three volunteers—Michael Schwerner, Andy Goodman, and James Chaney—disap-

In Mississippi only whites were allowed to join the Democratic Party, so as part of the 1964 Freedom Summer program, Fannie Lou Hamer helped to create a new political party, the Mississippi Freedom Democratic Party (MFDP). People of any race could join, but most MFDP members were African American.

peared. Their bodies were found buried together almost two months later. They had been murdered.

Those murders, and others, frightened other volunteers. During Freedom Summer, six people were murdered, 35 shootings were reported, at least 80 volunteers were beaten, and over 1,000 people were arrested. More than 60 churches, homes, or black-owned businesses were bombed or burned. But the violent attacks didn't stop the activists.

The Freedom Summer program didn't achieve all its goals, but it would make a big difference in the lives of African Americans in Mississippi. By 1969, the number of registered black voters had risen to more than 66 percent.

CIVIL RIGHTS LEGISLATION PASSES

In the summer of 1963 President Kennedy had proposed civil rights legislation, but he did not live to see it passed by Congress. After Kennedy's assassination in November 1963, his successor, President Lyndon B. Johnson, made sure that the proposed bill would become law.

The Civil Rights Act of 1964, which Johnson signed on July 2, outlawed discrimination based on an individual's race, color, religion, sex, or national origin. The Act outlawed segregation in businesses such as theaters, restaurants, and hotels. It banned discriminatory practices in hiring, promoting, setting wages, and firing employees. And it outlawed segregation in public facilities such as swimming pools, libraries, and public schools.

The Civil Rights Act was a major step, but it was not enough. Activists wanted another federal law that would ensure voting rights for African Americans. Public support for this law increased after police brutally broke up a voting rights march in Alabama. On March 7, 1965, 600 civil rights protesters began a march from Selma to the state capital of Montgomery. They were attacked with billy clubs and tear gas. The day became known as Bloody Sunday.

On March 21, around 3,000 marchers led by Martin Luther King Jr., set out again. This time, participants in the Selma to Montgomery march

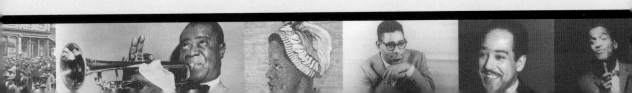

An Alternative to Nonviolence: Black Power

Not all African-American activists believed in nonviolence. One of those who didn't was Malcolm X (1925-1965). Malcolm X was a member of an African-American religious group called the Nation of Islam. He was a powerful speaker. His words and ideas excited many young African Americans. He made them proud to be black.

Malcolm X thought nonviolence was fine—if it worked. But if it didn't, then he thought black people should fight back against oppression. In one of his speeches, he said, "Be peaceful, be courteous, obey the law, respect everyone; but if someone puts his hand on you, send him to the cemetery."

Malcolm X didn't believe that white people would ever grant blacks equality. The solution, he thought, was for blacks to create their own society, separate from that of whites. Others came to feel the same way. In 1966 Stokely Carmichael, the head of the Student Nonviolent Coordinating Committee, began to use the term "Black Power" to describe this idea.

Malcolm X

The Black Power movement was confrontational. Its leaders spoke out against predominantly white-controlled state and local governments and their police departments. Supporters of Black Power were not afraid to use the tactics that whites had used against civil rights marchers. They bombed courthouses and government buildings, and fought back when police tried to arrest them. The encouraged riots as a way to express black anger about racist police forces and discrimination in housing and employment.

One of the most notorious Black Power groups was the Black Panther Party, which was founded by Bobby Seale and Huey Newton in 1966. Although the Black Panthers were known for their confrontations with police, they also established schools, medical clinics, and social programs to help poor African Americans in urban areas.

President Lyndon B. Johnson signs the 1965 Voting Rights Act. Watching are many civil rights leaders, including Dr. Martin Luther King, NAACP president Roy Wilkins, Vivian Malone, and Rosa Parks.

were escorted by the Alabama National Guard. On March 25, when the marchers reached the state capital, they numbered 25,000.

The news media reported on the voting rights march. And there was growing public support to remove obstacles that prevented blacks from voting. That August, Congress passed the Voting Rights Act. It called for federal workers to register black voters. And it prohibited the use of the literacy test as a condition for voting. On August 6, 1965, President Johnson signed the Voting Rights Act into law.

As a result, the number of African-Americans registered to vote soared throughout the nation. By the end of 1965, a quarter of a million new black voters had been registered.

As African Americans gained political power, many ran for elected office. In 1968 Shirley Chisholm became the first African American woman to win a seat in Congress. She was elected to the House of Representatives, from New York. In 1972 she ran for the Democratic nomination for president of the United States.

STILL WORK TO BE DONE

Passage of federal legislation ensuring that African Americans would have the same rights as whites was the crowning achievement of the Civil Rights Movement. However, black activists did not stop once the laws were passed. They continued working to make sure that the rights of black Americans were protected.

In 1965, the Southern Christian Leadership Conference turned its attention north to the city of Chicago, where blacks were often not permitted to buy houses in white neighborhoods. Martin Luther King and others fought for open housing as well as access to better education and jobs. King also spoke out on other issues that affected African Americans, such as poverty and the escalating war in Vietnam.

In March 1968 King traveled to Memphis, Tennessee, where he met with garbage collectors who were refusing to work because they wanted better pay and improved working conditions. While in Memphis, on April 4, 1968, King stood on the balcony of a hotel room he was sharing with his friend Ralph Abernathy. A shot rang out—a white man named James Earl Ray had shot King. His death led to riots in more than 100 U.S. cities.

ACCOMPLISHMENTS OF THE MOVEMENT

The struggle for African American civil rights was long and painful. But by the late 1960s, Jim Crow was gone. The Civil Rights and Voting Rights Acts made discrimination illegal. Blacks in the South could vote without fear, and many more were registering. African Americans were running in local, state, and national races—and getting elected.

African-American civil rights activists had succeeded. But the struggle wasn't over. Racism and discrimination still existed in the United States, even if they were not as obvious as in the past. There was still work to be done. After the death of Martin Luther King, people like Jesse Jackson, Ralph Abernathy, Julian Bond, John Lewis, and others continued the struggle to ensure African-American civil rights.

Many people who took part in the Civil Rights Movements were overjoyed on January 20, 2009, when Barack Obama was inaugurated as the first African-American president of the United States. However, serious problems remain for African Americans today. Many blacks are poor and are poorly educated. A high percentage of young African-American men are in prison, many on drug-related charges.

The Civil Rights Movement of the 1950s and 1960s has helped to shape American history over the past five decades. The heroes of that movement proved that even the most challenging problems can be overcome, through bravery, hard work, and a willingness to keep fighting to ensure that every American is treated equally and with dignity.

CHAPTER NOTES

p. 13: "We hold these Truths . . ." Declaration of Independence. http://www.archives.gov/exhibits/charters/declaration_transcript.html

p. 15: "involuntary servitude" Thirteenth Amendment to the U.S. Constitution (1865). http://www.ourdocuments.gov/doc.php?flash=true&doc=40

p. 15: "White men alone . . ." Carol Berkin et al., *Making America: A History of the United States. Volume 1: To 1877* (Stamford, Conn.: Cengage Learning, 2007), p. 441.

p. 17: "all persons within . . ." Civil Rights Act of 1875, cited at *Reconstruction: The Second Civil War*, PBS American Experience. http://www.pbs.org/wgbh/amex/reconstruction/activism/ps_1875.html

p. 19: "was undoubtedly to enforce . . ." *Plessy v. Ferguson*, 163 U.S. 537 (1896). http://caselaw.lp.findlaw.com/scripts/getcase.pl?court=us&vol=163&invol=537

p. 19: "could not have been intended . . ." Ibid.

p. 24: "It is hereby declared . . ." Harry S. Truman, Executive Order 9981. http://www.trumanlibrary.org/photos/9981a.jpg

p. 26: "segregation of white and colored . . ." *Brown v. Board of Education*, 347 U.S. 483 (1954). http://caselaw.lp.findlaw.com/cgi-bin/getcase.pl?court=US&vol=347&invol=483

p. 27: "everybody needed to know . . ." Mamie Till Mobley, quoted in *American Experience: The Murder of Emmett Till*, PBS (2003). http://www.pbs.org/wgbh/amex/till/filmmore/pt.html

p. 30: "Let me have those seats . . ." Rosa Parks with Jim Haskins, *Rosa Parks: My Story* (New York: Dial Books, 1992), p. 86.

p. 30: "I could not see how . . ." Ibid.

p. 30: "I'm going to have you arrested . . ." Ibid.

p. 30: "Why do you all push us around?" Ibid., p. 116.

p. 31: "We had to make it clear . . ." Martin Luther King Jr., "The Power of Non-violence" (June 4, 1957). http://teachingamericanhistory.org/library/index.asp?document=1131

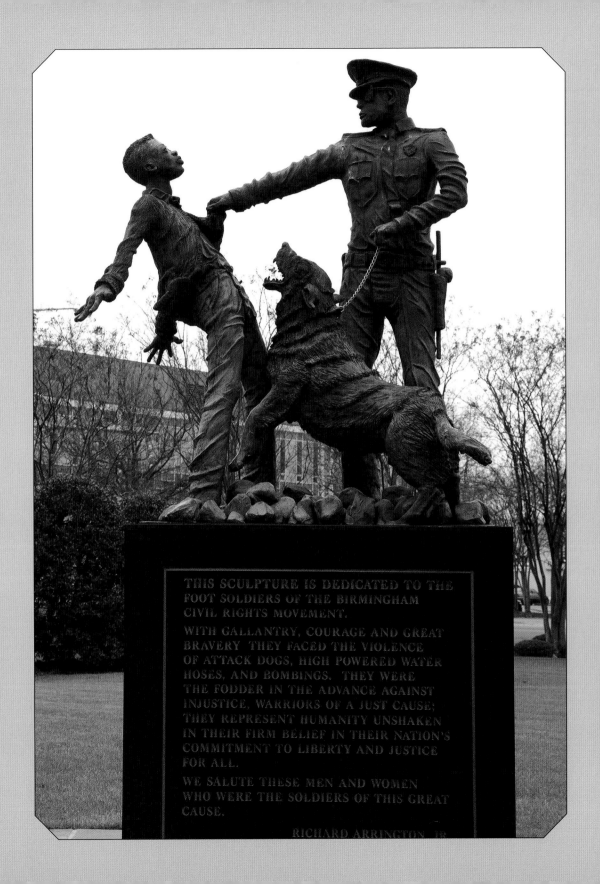

THIS SCULPTURE IS DEDICATED TO THE
FOOT SOLDIERS OF THE BIRMINGHAM
CIVIL RIGHTS MOVEMENT.

WITH GALLANTRY, COURAGE AND GREAT
BRAVERY THEY FACED THE VIOLENCE
OF ATTACK DOGS, HIGH POWERED WATER
HOSES, AND BOMBINGS. THEY WERE
THE FODDER IN THE ADVANCE AGAINST
INJUSTICE, WARRIORS OF A JUST CAUSE;
THEY REPRESENT HUMANITY UNSHAKEN
IN THEIR FIRM BELIEF IN THEIR NATION'S
COMMITMENT TO LIBERTY AND JUSTICE
FOR ALL.

WE SALUTE THESE MEN AND WOMEN
WHO WERE THE SOLDIERS OF THIS GREAT
CAUSE.

RICHARD ARRINGTON, JR.

p. 32: "I want it to be known . . ." Martin Luther King Jr., *The Papers of Martin Luther King Jr. Volume III: Birth of a New Age*, edited by Clayborne Carson (Berkeley and Los Angeles: University of California Press, 1997), p. 73.

p. 37: "They symbolized a change . . ." James Farmer, quoted in Jim Schlosser, "Greensboro Sit-ins: Launch of a Civil Rights Movement," *Greensboro News and Record*. http://www.sitins.com/story.shtml

p. 37: "When the students . . ." Diane Nash, quoted in Juan Williams, *Eyes on the Prize* (New York: Penguin Books, 1987), p. 129.

p. 38: "Mayor West, do you feel . . ." Lynne Olson, *Freedom's Daughters: The Unsung Heroines of the Civil Rights Movement from 1830 to 1970* (New York: Scribner, 2001), p. 159.

p. 40: "If the Freedom Riders . . ." Diane Nash, quoted in *Eyes on the Prize: America's Civil Rights Movement, 1954-1985*, PBS. http://www.pbs.org/wgbh/amex/eyesontheprize/about/pt_103.html

p. 43: "I say segregation now . . ." George Wallace, "Inaugural Address" (January 14, 1963). http://www.archives.alabama.gov/govs_list/inauguralspeech.html

p. 44: "You express a great deal . . ." Martin Luther King Jr., "Letter from a Birmingham Jail," in *A Testament of Hope: The Essential Writings and Speeches of Martin Luther King*, edited by James M. Washington (New York: HarperCollins, 1986), p. 293.

p. 45-46: "I have a dream that . . ." Martin Luther King Jr., "I Have a Dream" (August 28, 1963). http://www.americanrhetoric.com/speeches/mlkihaveadream.htm

p. 50: "Be peaceful, be courteous . . ." Malcolm X, *Malcolm X Speaks: Selected Speeches and Statements*, edited by George Breitman (New York: Grove Press, 1965), p. 12.

CHRONOLOGY

1941: President Franklin D. Roosevelt signs the Fair Employment Act into law on June 25. It orders companies working for the United States to treat all workers and job-seekers fairly, including African Americans.

1947: Bayard Rustin organizes the "Journey of Reconciliation," a bus trip by black and white activists through Virginia, North Carolina, Tennessee, and Kentucky to challenge segregation. This action inspired the Freedom Rides of 1961.

1948: President Harry Truman issues Executive Order 9981 on July 26, desegregating the U.S. armed forces.

1954: In May, the Supreme Court rules in *Brown v. Board of Education* that segregation of public schools is unconstitutional; it orders schools to desegregate "with all deliberate speed."

1955: The murder of Emmett Till in Mississippi in August, and the subsequent acquittal of the teenager's murders, draws national attention to the plight of African Americans in the Deep South; on December 1, Rosa Parks is arrested for refusing to give a white passenger her seat on a Montgomery, Alabama, bus. Five days later African Americans begin a boycott of Montgomery buses that lasts until late 1956, when the U.S. Supreme Court rules that racial segregation on public buses is illegal.

1957: In September nine African-American students begin school at Central High School in Little Rock, Arkansas. U.S. troops are sent to protect them from angry mobs of whites opposed to desegregation.

1960: Four African-American students ask for service at the "white" section of a lunch counter in Greensboro, North Carolina, and are refused. This sparks student "sit-ins" across the South.

1961: CORE and SNCC send racially integrated groups of "Freedom Riders" on bus trips in the South, beginning May 4, 1961, in Washington, D.C. The riders are met with force in many communities.

1963: On August 28, approximately 250,000 people participate in a major civil rights rally in Washington, D.C. As part of the events, Dr. Martin Luther King Jr. delivers his "I Have a Dream" speech. On September 15, a bomb explodes at the 16th Street Baptist Church in Birmingham, killing four young girls and injuring 22.

1964:   On July 2, President Lyndon B. Johnson signs the Civil Rights Act into law. This historic legislation prohibits discrimination and racial segregation in schools, workplaces, and public facilities. In Mississippi, Freedom Summer activities lead to a surge in voter registration.

1965:   In February, Malcolm X is assassinated; on August 6, President Johnson signs the Voting Rights Act, making it illegal for states to prevent African Americans from voting by the use of poll taxes, literacy tests, or other means.

1967:   Thurgood Marshall becomes the first African-American to serve as a United States Supreme Court judge on June 13.

1968:   On April 4 Dr. Martin Luther King Jr. is assassinated in Memphis, Tennessee. Riots break out in cities across the United States. On April 11, President Johnson signs the Fair Housing Act, which bans discrimination in the sale, rental, and financing of housing.

Both blacks and whites take part in one of the 1965 marches from Selma to Montgomery, Alabama, which were held to encourage African Americans to vote.

GLOSSARY

abolitionist—a person favoring the end of slavery.

amendment—a change made to a constitution or law.

boycott—to refuse to associate with, buy the products of, or use the services of a company or organization as a means of protest.

civil disobedience—to disobey a law because of a belief that the law is wrong, and with a willingness to accept punishment as a consequence in order to set an example to others.

civil rights—the rights to political and social freedom and equality.

desegregate—to end a policy of racial segregation.

discrimination—unfair treatment of a person based on that person's race, gender, social class, or other characteristic.

integrate—to include people from all races.

Jim Crow—a term for southern laws created after the Reconstruction period, which restricted the rights of African Americans.

lynch—to put someone to death outside of the law, through mob action.

oppression—the unjust or cruel use of power.

segregation—the practice of keeping one group or race separated from another.

Reconstruction—the period from 1865 to 1877 when the southern states were re-admitted to the United States after the Civil War. During this period slavery ended and blacks gained the rights of citizenship.

white supremacist—a white person who believes that white people are superior to people of other racial backgrounds.

FURTHER READING

Alexander, Michelle. *The New Jim Crow: Mass Incarceration in the Age of Colorblindness*. New York: The New Press, 2010.

Aretha, David. *Sit-ins and Freedom Rides*. Greensboro, N.C.: Morgan Reynolds Publishing, 2009.

Cashin, Sheryll. *The Failures Of Integration: How Race and Class Are Undermining the American Dream*. Cambridge, Mass.: Perseus Books Group, 2004.

D'Emilio, John. *Lost Prophet: The life and Times of Bayard Rustin*. New York: Free Press, 2003.

Fitzgerald, Stephanie. *Little Rock Nine: Struggle for Integration*. Minneapolis: Compass Point Books, 2006.

Freedman, Russell. *Freedom Walkers: The Story of the Montgomery Bus Boycott*. New York: Holiday House Publishers, 2008.

Garrow, David. *Bearing the Cross: Martin Luther King and the Southern Christian Leadership Conference*. New York: Morrow, 1986.

Hardy, Sheila Jackson, and P. Stephen Hardy. *Extraordinary People of the Civil Rights Movement*. Danbury, Conn.: Children's Press, 2007.

Hasday, Judy L. *Women in the Civil Rights Movement*. Philadelphia: Mason Crest, 2012.

Henderson, Cheryl Brown, "Lucinda Todd and the Invisible Petitioners of *Brown v. Board of Education of Topeka, Kansas*" in Quintard Taylor and Shirley Ann Wilson Moore, eds., *African American Women Confront the West: 1600-2000*. Norman:University of Oklahoma Press, 2003.

McAdam, Doug. *Freedom Summer*. New York: Oxford University Press, 1988.

Phibbs, Cheryl Fisher. *The Montgomery Bus Boycott: A History and Reference Guide*. Santa Barbara, Calif.: ABC-CLIO, 2009.

Robnett, Belinda. *How long? How long?: African-American Women in the Struggle for Civil Rights*. New York: Oxford University Press, 1997.

Rodriguez, Junius P. *Slavery in the United States: A Social, Political, and Historical Encyclopedia*, Vol. 2. Santa Barbara, Calif.: ABC-CLIO, 2007.

INTERNET RESOURCES

http://www.jimcrowhistory.org/history/creating.htm

This site links to several essays on American society during the Jim Crow years. It also gives various individual's perspectives on how Jim Crow affected their lives.

http://www.loc.gov/exhibits/brown/

Hosted by the Library of Congress, this website revisits the *Brown v. Board of Education* ruling. The site features photos of people and documents relating to the years before and after the 1954 order to desegregate public schools.

http://www.morethanabusride.org

The website for the film *More Than a Bus Ride* provides background information on civil rights activist Jo Ann Robinson and the women plaintiffs in the class action lawsuit *Browder v. Gayle*.

http://www.pbs.org/wgbh/amex/eyesontheprize

Based on the PBS American Experience television series *Eyes on the Prize: America's Civil Rights Movement 1954–1985*, this site links to profiles on people and documents from the time.

http://www.pbs.org/wnet/jimcrow

This website provides background information on segregation in the United States and Jim Crow laws. Includes maps and activities.

http://www.rosaparks.org

This official website of the Rosa and Raymond Parks Institute for Self Development provides information on the institute and a detailed biography of Rosa Parks.

INDEX

Numbers in **bold italics** refer to captions.

CONTRIBUTORS

M. LAVORA PERRY wrote *Taneesha Never Disparaging*, a funny story about a fifth grader facing a teen bully on the street and an imaginary but loud evil twin. *Teaching for Change* called *Taneesha Never Disparaging* "A Must-Read." Ms. Perry lives in Ohio with her husband and three children. She likes bicycling and stands while she writes.

Senior Consulting Editor **DR. MARC LAMONT HILL** is one of the leading hip-hop generation intellectuals in the country. Dr. Hill has lectured widely and provides regular commentary for media outlets like NPR, the *Washington Post, Essence Magazine*, the *New York Times*, CNN, MSNBC, and *The O'Reilly Factor*. He is the host of the nationally syndicated television show *Our World With Black Enterprise*. Dr. Hill is a columnist and editor-at-large for the *Philadelphia Daily News*. His books include the award-winning *Beats, Rhymes, and Classroom Life: Hip-Hop Pedagogy and the Politics of Identity* (2009).

Since 2009 Dr. Hill has been on the faculty of Columbia University as Associate Professor of Education at Teachers College. He holds an affiliated faculty appointment in African American Studies at the Institute for Research in African American Studies at Columbia University.

Since his days as a youth in Philadelphia, Dr. Hill has been a social justice activist and organizer. He is a founding board member of My5th, a non-profit organization devoted to educating youth about their legal rights and responsibilities. He is also a board member and organizer of the Philadelphia Student Union. Dr. Hill also works closely with the ACLU Drug Reform Project, focusing on drug informant policy. In addition to his political work, Dr. Hill continues to work directly with African American and Latino youth.

In 2005, *Ebony* named Dr. Hill one of America's 100 most influential Black leaders. The magazine had previously named him one of America's top 30 Black leaders under 30 years old.